·THE· HISTRONAUTS

AN EGYPTIAN ADVENTURE

Written by
FRANCES DURKIN

Illustrated by
GRACE COOKE

Designed by
VICKY BARKER

www.bsmall.co.uk

Meet
The Histronauts

Luna

Age: Eight years
Likes: History, adventures, animals, problem solving and storytelling
Dislikes: Getting lost and bad smells
Favourite Colour: Blue
Favourite Food: Beans on toast
Favourite Place: Castles

Nani

Age: Seven and a half years
Likes: Science, nature, maths, gardening, flowers and exploring
Dislikes: People who don't recycle
Favourite Colour: Green
Favourite Food: Anything green
Favourite Place: Anywhere outside but mostly forests

Newton

Age: Ten years
Likes: Making things, eating, reading, cooking and playing games
Dislikes: Being hungry and being cold
Favourite Colour: Yellow
Favourite Food: Everything!
Favourite Place: Home

Hero

Age: Five years
Likes: Sleeping, being Luna's cat
Dislikes: Getting wet
Favourite Food: Chicken
Favourite Place: Curled up on the sofa

Contents

The Histronauts visit a museum

The Histronauts are taking a trip to the museum on a very cold and rainy day.

I can't wait to see the exhibition about ancient Egypt.

This is our stop. Nani, press the bell.

EGYPT

It looks amazing!

NO BUBBLE GUM
NO BANANAS
NO RUNNING
NO LOUD SNEEZES
NO JIGSAW PUZZLES
NO SMELLY FEET
NO CATS

Oh no! Hero will have to wait outside.

But it's raining!

Sorry Luna.

But...

NO BUBBLE GUM
NO BANANAS
NO RUNNING
NO LOUD SNEEZES
NO JIGSAW PUZZLES
NO SMELLY FEET

Wait for us here Hero.

Inside the museum

Map of
Ancient Egypt
5000 BC – 30 BC

Archaeology

- This is the excavation of historical sites and the study of ancient objects.
- People who practise archaeology are called archaeologists.
- Archaeologists study these places and things to learn about how people used to live.
- Many ancient Egyptian sites have been discovered by archaeologists.

Timeline

3800-3100 BC
Predynastic Period
The first settlers farmed the land alongside the Nile.

3100-2686 BC
Early Dynastic Period
Egypt has two parts: Upper Egypt and Lower Egypt.

2686-2181 BC
Old Kingdom
One ruler unites the two parts of Egypt and builds the Great Pyramids at Giza.

2181-2025 BC
First Intermediate Period
The Old Kingdom ends and Egypt divides again.

2025-1700 BC
Middle Kingdom
Egypt reunites and becomes a powerful centre for the development of the arts and science.

1700-1550 BC
Second Intermediate Period
The kingdom divides and Upper Egypt is invaded by the Hyksos.

1550-1069 BC
New Kingdom
Once again one ruler unites Egypt. It becomes very powerful. The pharaohs are now buried in the Valley of the Kings.

1069-664 BC
Third Intermediate Period
Libyan and Nubian invaders divide Egypt.

664-332 BC
Late Period
Egypt reclaims its independence.

332-30 BC
Ptolemaic Period
Alexander the Great invades Egypt and places his general Ptolemy in charge.

69 BC
Egypt's final pharaoh, Cleopatra VII, is born.

30 BC
Cleopatra VII dies and Egypt becomes a part of the Roman Empire.

Red Sea

Lower Egypt

Cairo
(Modern day capital)

Amarna
(Akhetaten)
Capital city around 1353-1332 BC

Nile river

Giza
(Site of the Pyramids)
2700-1700 BC

Memphis
(Men-nefer)
Capital city around 2613-2181 BC

Alexandria
Founded around 331 BC

Luxor
(Waset)
Thebes to the
ancient Romans

Philae
Founded
around 380 BC

Deir el-Medina
(Set Maat)
Existed from around
1550-1080 BC

Upper Egypt

Did you know?

- The Nile Delta is where the river meets the Mediterranean Sea.

- Every year between June and September the river floods.

- The flood waters leave nutrients in the soil and make it excellent for farming.

- During the Old Kingdom, the capital of Egypt was called Memphis.

- The capital during the Middle and New Kingdoms was called Thebes.

Ancient Egyptian paper

- The ancient Egyptians have made paper from papyrus since around 4000 BC.

- The plant can grow up to 5 metres (6 and a half feet) high.

- Papyrus reeds are also used to make boats, baskets and sandals.

- Even the ancient Romans used papyrus.

- Parchment, made from animals' skins, eventually took the place of papyrus.

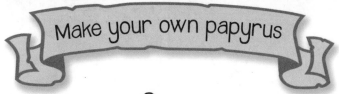

Make your own papyrus

You will need:

- Paper

- Scissors

- Glue

1. Imagine that the paper is a papyrus reed and cut it into strips.

2. Lay half of the strips next to each other horizontally (side by side).

3. Cover the top side of these strips with glue.

4. Take the other half of the strips and place them vertically (top to bottom) on top of the glue.

5. Wait for the glue to dry and you have your own papyrus to write on.

13

14

As the group walk along, they pass a field full of farmers harvesting barley.

Ancient Egyptian seasons

- **Akhet** (June-September) is when the Nile floods.

- **Peret** (October-February) is when the floodwaters recede and the soil can be ploughed and planted with seeds.

- **Shemu** (March-May) is when the farmers harvest the crops.

So we are here during 'Shemu'.

Those farmers must be really hot!

The men working in the water must be much cooler!

It all looks like very hard work to me.

Calendar and seasons

As well as having three seasons, the Egyptian year is made of 12 months. Each month has three weeks. Each week has ten days. The ancient Egyptians use sundials to tell the time during the day.

What's a sundial, Luna?

It's a sort of clock. As the sun moves from east to west it casts a shadow on the sundial and shows what the time is.

That's very clever!

Make a sundial

You will need:

- Cardboard
- Scissors
- Glue
- A compass

1. Copy the templates on the opposite page on to the cardboard and cut them out.

2. Glue the 'gnomon' (triangle) into the marked place on the centre line of the base.

3. The gnomon shoul stand upright on the base.

4. When the sun is shining, take the sundial outside.

5. Using the compass find north and align the arrow on the base with the compass.

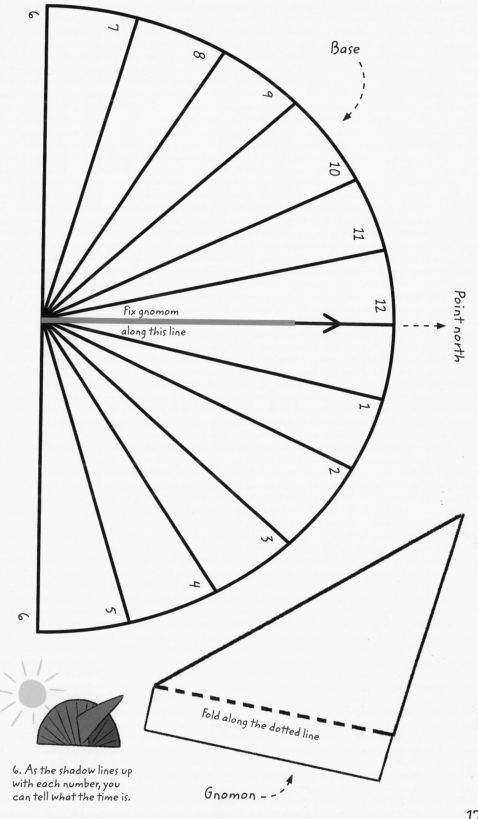

6

7

8

9

10

11

12

1

2

3

4

5

6

Base

Point north

Fix gnomom
along this line

Fold along the dotted line

Gnomon

6. As the shadow lines up
with each number, you
can tell what the time is.

Is that why those guards are there?

They look scary!

People called pharaohs rule ancient Egypt. When the pharaohs die they are buried in secret tombs. Inside all tombs people are buried with the possessions they might need for their afterlife. Pharaohs are also buried with gold and riches that will make their afterlife luxurious.

Yes. They stop thieves from stealing from the tombs.

All about pyramids

- The pyramids are magnificent triangle-shaped structures.

- They are made of heavy blocks of sandstone in a place called Giza.

- Slaves are not used to build the pyramids. Farmers build the pyramids and they are paid to work during the season when the Nile floods their farmland.

- It is very difficult work but the people believe that they are working to please the Pharaoh.

- Pyramids are very big and very easy for thieves to see from far away.

- Everybody knows that these tombs contain gold and riches. This means that they are easy for robbers to find.

- Thieves started breaking into the pyramids and stealing the treasures.

Now we bury our pharaohs in tombs here in the Valley of the Kings. These tombs are a secret and the people who build them live in a village nearby. We call this village Set Maat which means 'Place of Truth'. We have been building tombs here for hundreds of years and many generations of families have worked on them. My grandfather was the craftsman who painted the burial mask of King Tutankhamen.

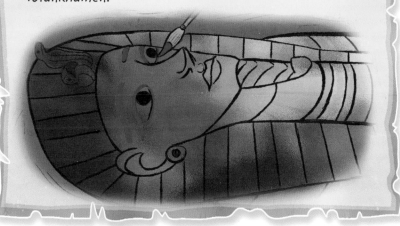

Can we visit Set Maat?

Well, maybe. It's just the other side of the valley. But it is a secret and if the guards see you, they will send you away.

That's such a shame!

But...today our food is being delivered from Waset.

If we can sneak through the tombs to the other side without being seen, we might be able to slip in to Set Maat with the delivery.

Let's try it!

I'm not so sure. Those guards look very frightening!

The secret of Set Maat

Find your way through the maze and avoid all of the obstacles.

Entrance to
the city

Set Maat

- This village is home to around 100 people.

- The people who live here work on the tombs in the Valley of the Kings.

- These craftsmen include stonemasons, carpenters, potters, basket-makers and artists.

- Some people work inside their homes to make the objects that go in the tombs.

- Other groups of workers go out to the valley to build and decorate the tombs.

- The workers are split into two groups who work on opposite walls of the tombs.

- Their salary is a ration of water, oils, beer, grain, firewood, clothing and pottery.

- A working week lasts for eight days followed by two days holiday.

- On their days off they work on their own tombs and can use their skills to earn extra money.

No, but we make things for the mummies here.

Mask-maker

- The pharaohs buried in the Valley of the Kings wear death masks.

- These royal masks are made from precious metals such as gold and bronze.

- Poorer people are buried in masks which are made of **cartonnage**. This is linen or papyrus which has been soaked in water and dried onto a wooden mould.

- Temple priests wear cartonnage ritual masks which look like the animal heads of the gods of ancient Egypt.

This is the jewellery maker's workshop. I need to collect my new necklace.

- Ancient Egyptians wear earrings, rings, necklaces, bracelets, armbands and anklets.

- Jewellers use copper, gold and precious gems such as emeralds, pearls, quartz, garnet and lapis lazuli for their work.

- The Egyptians also make glass beads from ground quartz which is mixed with chemicals and heated to form the shape they want to make.

Make your Egyptian necklace

You will need:

- Cardboard
- A large plate
- A small plate
- Scissors
- Things to decorate the necklace, e.g. beads, shells, pasta, paints.

1. Draw around the large plate onto the cardboard.

2. Draw around the small plate inside the larger plate's outline, closer to the top edge like in the picture.

3. Cut out the two circles and cut a small chunk from the thin side so that it will fit around your neck.

4. You then have a necklace which you can decorate however you like.

Are you all ready to see my husband at work?

Yes!

An ancient Egyptian home

Niche

Altar

Reception room

At home in ancient Egypt

- Ancient Egyptians make their houses from mud-brick.

- Many of the houses in Set Maat have a shrine and a workshop.

- The houses also have underground cellars for keeping food cool.

- The kitchens have a domed oven for baking.

Stored grains

Bedroom

Kitchen

Cellar

- There are no bathrooms inside the houses of Set Maat. Residents go outside to use a toilet stool with a ceramic bowl underneath.

- Instead of pillows, ancient Egyptians use headrests. They have several beds in one room.

- Houses are lit by lamps which usually burnt olive oil.

34

Hieroglyphic symbols

Our writing is called hieroglyphics and our alphabet contains over 700 different characters. There are no punctuation marks and sometimes we write left to right, right to left, top to bottom or bottom to top. You can tell which way it's going because the animal symbols face that way. We write on papyrus with pens made from reeds. We sharpen the reeds and dip them into ink which is made from plant minerals mixed with oil or honey.

Sky		Hand	
Water		Sun	
Eye		House	
Foot		Beetle	
Bull		Owl	

The ancient Egyptians use symbols to represent certain spoken sounds, just like our alphabet.
We call these hieroglyphic sound symbols phonograms.
A symbol which represents a whole word or a phrase is called a logogram. The ancient Egyptians don't write their vowel sounds so it is difficult to know exactly how they pronounce their words.
The hieroglyphic alphabet below shows the Egyptian phonograms which are similar to the alphabet you know.

Use this alphabet to write your own name.
Use this code to write secret messages to your friends.

Translate this page. What does it say?
Don't forget to read in the direction in which
the animals are facing.

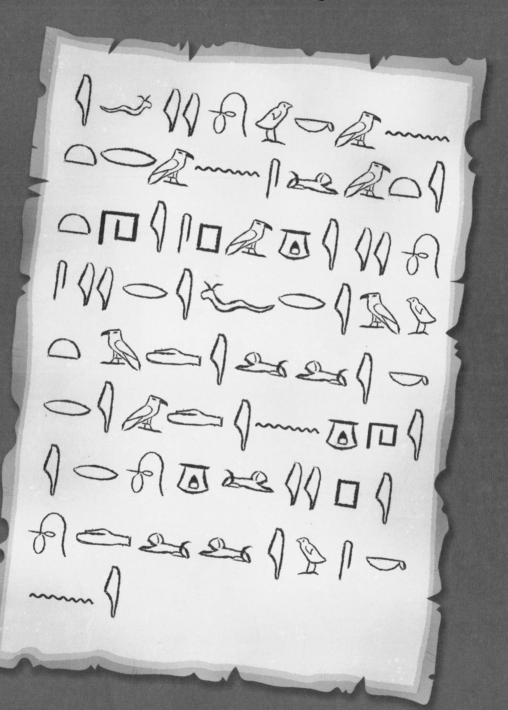

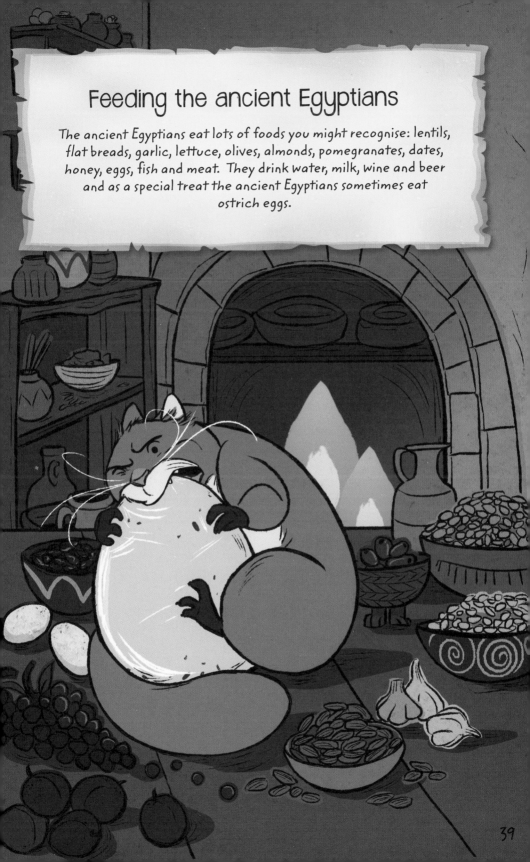

Feeding the ancient Egyptians

The ancient Egyptians eat lots of foods you might recognise: lentils, flat breads, garlic, lettuce, olives, almonds, pomegranates, dates, honey, eggs, fish and meat. They drink water, milk, wine and beer and as a special treat the ancient Egyptians sometimes eat ostrich eggs.

Recipe for Egyptian flat bread

Ingredients:
300 ml warm water
25 g fresh yeast
500 g spelt flour
1/2 tsp. salt

Mix the yeast and water together in a bowl.
Gradually add the flour and the salt to make a dough.
Cover with a damp tea towel and leave it to rise until
it's double its size.
Preheat the oven to 200°C (180°C for fan ovens). Ask an
adult for help when using the oven.
Sprinkle some flour on the work surface and knead the dough.
Divide the dough into eight pieces and press them flat
(about 1 cm thick).
Put onto a baking tray and bake for 10 minutes.
Let them cool.

Enjoy!

Recipe for tiger nut sweets

This recipe was found written on a piece of broken pottery dating back to 1600 BC.

Ingredients:
400 g fresh pitted dates
2 tbsp. water
2 tbsp. cinnamon powder
1/2 tsp. cardamom powder
4 tbsp. roughly chopped walnuts
Some runny honey
4 tbsp. finely chopped almonds

Mash the dates with the water and then add the cinnamon, cardamom and walnuts.
Mix the ingredients together and roll into balls.
Cover in honey and roll the sticky balls into the chopped almonds.
Put them into the fridge to chill for an hour. Yum!

Did you know?

The ancient Egyptians eat with their hands and dip their fingers into a little bowl of water to clean them. They sit on mats on the floor around a bowl of food and take turns dipping their bread into it. Once that bowl is empty, another course comes out for them to enjoy.

How to play senet

You will need:

14 counters (seven counters each of two different colours)
Four throw sticks which are plain on one side and coloured on the other.
(You can make these out of lollipop sticks or strips of card.)

Four decorated or plain sides scores 5	Three plain surfaces scores 3	Two plain surfaces scores 2	One plain surface scores 1

- Place the counters on the board one colour after the other on the first 14 spaces.

- Each player takes turns throwing all four sticks at once.

- Move each piece according to the score you have thrown.

- If you land on the other player's counter, swap places.

- If you land on your own counter, throw again.

- Square 15 is called the House of Rebirth and it is the starting square.

- Square 26 is called The House of Happiness. You cannot jump over this and must throw the right score to land land directly on it before you can move on.

- Square 27 is called the House of Water. If you land here you must go back to Square 15.

- Square 28 is called The House of the Three Truths. You can only leave this square if you throw a three.

- Square 29 is called The House of Re-Atoum. You can only leave this square if you throw a two.

The winner is the first to clear all their counters off the board.

Keeping up appearances

- The ancient Egyptians take great pride in their appearance.

- Men and women wear make-up as a sign of their status.

- They create make-up by grinding together different natural minerals and pigments.

- Black eye make-up called **kohl** is very popular.

- They paint their cheeks and lips with a red mineral called ochre, which comes from clay.

- People in ancient Egypt colour their hair and paint their nails with a dye called henna.

More than meets the eye

- Make-up is not just important for appearances but also for medicinal and magical reasons.

- **Kohl** is thought to protect the eyes from the sun, from infections and flies.

- Some green eye make-up is thought to be a symbol of the god of the sky and the sun, Horus.

- The Egyptians have doctors and take medicines when unwell.

- Those medicines are made of plants, oils and juices.

In the house of the goddess

Throughout Egypt, temples are built as houses for the gods.
Each temple is dedicated to a specific god and inside there is a room
called the sanctuary. In the sanctuary there is a shrine which has a
door and behind that door there is a statue of the god.
Every day the temple priests and priestesses worship at
the shrine of the god.

Would you like to give something to the goddess?

Rituals

- Worshippers give offerings of food to the god of the temple.

- Ceremonies of worship take place in the temple every day.

- As well as the daily rituals there are also regular festivals at specific times of the year.

- Some temples even keep sacred animals.

- The cow sometimes represents the goddess Hathor.

Uh, there's a cow in here.

Egyptian gods

There are lots of Egyptian gods.

Isis

Status:

Goddess of nature and magic

Appearance:

Headdress shaped like a throne

The wife of Osiris and the mother of Horus

Ra

Status:

God of the sun

Appearance:

Head of a hawk and sun disk

It was thought that Ra was swallowed by the sky goddess every night and reborn each morning

Osiris

Status:

God of the underworld and the dead

Appearance:

Headdress shaped like a cone (atef) with feathers. He carries a crook and flail

Osiris was killed by his brother Set and became lord of the underworld

Anubis

Status:

God of mummification

Appearance:

Head of a jackal

He guided the dead into the afterlife

- There are more than 2,000 ancient Egyptian gods.

- The Egyptians believe pharaohs to be living gods.

Bastet

Status:
Goddess of protection

Appearance:
Head of a cat

Traditionally the protector of the pharaoh

Thoth

Status:
God of Wisdom, writing and knowledge

Appearance:
Head of an ibis bird

The ancient Egyptians believed that hieroglyphs were a gift from Thoth

Horus

Status:
God of the sky

Appearance:
Head of a falcon

It was believed that the pharaoh was the living incarnation of Horus

Amun

Status:
God of creation

Appearance:
Head of a ram

The king of the gods

Hathor

Status:
Goddess of music, love and joy

Appearance:
Horns of a cow and sun disk

More festivals were dedicated to Hathor than any other gods

Sobek

Status:
God of the waterways

Appearance:
Head of a crocodile

Temples dedicated to Sobek frequently kept live crocodiles which the priests and priestesses mummified after their deaths

- Male gods have red/brown skin because they spend their time outside.

- Female gods have yellow skin because they spend their time indoors.

I know a story about some Egyptian gods.

The gods Osiris and Isis ruled Egypt together. They had a baby son named Horus. They were very happy and all of Egypt grew rich and prosperous. Osiris' brother Set became very jealous of all the power and success that he had.

One day Set tricked Osiris into climbing into a chest which he sealed shut and dropped into the Nile.

Isis wept at the loss of her husband and was so afraid for her son that she took the baby and ran away. Isis was upset that her husband had not been buried with the proper funeral ceremony and could not pass into the afterlife.

She journeyed for a long time looking for her husband. Eventually, she discovered the chest but Set found out and was very angry. This time, he broke the chest into fourteen pieces and scattered them all over Egypt. Isis began her search again and where she found each piece of his body, she immediately carried out the funeral rituals. Once she had found all fourteen pieces, Osiris was able to journey into the underworld where he became god of the afterlife.

When the baby Horus grew up, he became so powerful that he killed Set and became the new pharaoh of Egypt. It is said that after Horus died he continued to battle Set in the underworld and that when the battle is won, Osiris will be able to come back to the land of the living and become pharaoh again.

How clever of you to know that story.

Tia, what do you do for your job?

I am one of the priestesses here.

It is the job of the priests to carry out the daily rituals to worship the gods. They also track the hours of the day and the movement of the stars to decide the best time of year to plant the crops. I am one of the priestesses here and I play music and sing at the festivals.

What sort of festivals?

We celebrate the different gods. My favourite festival is called the Feast of Anket, which welcomes the rising of the Nile.

I play the **menit** and the **sistrum**.

What instrument do you play?

Frame drum

Drums are used for both military and religious purposes. Frame drums are round and held in one hand while they are beaten with the other.

Menit

The menit is a ceremonial neckla which the Egyptia use as a percussio instrument. It mak a rattle sound whe is shaken.

Flutes

The ancient Egyptians make flutes from long stalks of reed. They blow across the top of the reed and use finger holes to play different notes.

Barrel drum

Barrel drums are worn across the body and beaten with both hands. There is no evidence of the ancient Egyptians using drumsticks.

Sistrum

Sistrum means 'thing shaken'. This is a sacred musical instrument which is shaken to make a noise.

- Music is very important to the ancient Egyptians.

- They play many different types of musical instruments.

- Some music is played as part of religious rituals and prayers.

- Music is sometimes used as part of a magic spell (**heka**).

- Soldiers play drums and trumpets.

Sheneb

The ancient Egyptians play metal trumpets called Sheneb. They are made of silver or bronze and are decorated with colourful patterns. Two of these are found in the tomb of King Tutankhamen.

Clappers

Clappers are made of wood, ivory or bone and are beaten together to make a sound. Many are shaped like hands. They are the oldest known Egyptian instrument and date back to 3000 BC.

Harp

The harp is a stringed instrument which is played by plucking the strings to make a sound. They come in many different shapes and sizes.

55

"And now I must take this to the priest who will make the mummy."

"Inside their workshop, the mummification process happens very carefully."

"Wow. A real mummy!"

"I want to see."

"Mummification is very sacred so we're not allowed to see."

"I think I know a bit about how a mummy is made."

Ancient beliefs

- The Book of the Dead is a collection of magic spells that help a person pass through the underworld into the afterlife.

- It was developed around 1700 BC in Thebes.

- The book has 200 chapters.

- Before it is written on papyrus, the spells are written onto the walls of tombs and on **sarcophagi** (coffins).

Hero meets a mummy!

The body is placed onto a board and washed with water from the river Nile.

- Three people take part in the embalming process: a scribe, a cutter and an embalmer.

- The scribe supervises the cutter.

- The cutter makes the incisions into the body, but this job is considered unclean so is done by a member of the lower classes.

- The embalmer is a type of priest who dresses as the god Anubis to carry out mummification.

Once the organs have been removed the body is covered in **natron** (salt) and left to dry.

- After the forty days are over, the **natron** is washed off and the body is stuffed with sawdust, salt or linen. It is then sewn closed and given fake eyeballs.

After forty days the body is then covered with oils and has amulets placed upon it.

Types of Amulet

Scarab
meaning resurrection, transformation and protection.

Lotus
meaning the sun, creation and rebirth.

Ankh
means everlasting life.

Djed Pillar
(or 'Tet' amulet) representing stability and protection.

Eye of Horus
to protect and ward off evil.

Winged Isis
the goddess of rebirth

Circle of Ouroboros
represents renewal and unity.

They wrap the body in a layer of linen while a priest reads spells from the Book of the Dead.

The priests lay a cloth (shroud) with a picture of Osiris over the top of the body and bind it tightly with more linen.

Luna, you know so much about mummification! Should we be scared?

I wouldn't mummify you!

The next step is to place the burial mask on top of the body.

Finally the wrapped body is placed inside a coffin called a sarcophagus.

- A **sarcophagus** is made from reeds, pottery, wood or metal and decorated with enamel and precious jewels.

- The face of the person inside is painted onto the front of the coffin.

- The coffins are decorated with hieroglyphs of spells from the Book of the Dead.

- The **sarcophagus** of King Tutankhamen contains three coffins.

61

Hero, what happened?!

Is he yours? I'm so sorry. I was taking these offerings to the temple.

Offerings?

Yes. We offer mummified animals at the shrines to the gods.

People buy mummified animals from me to please their favourite gods.

Hero was nearly given to the gods?!

That's really strange. I'm glad we rescued you, Hero.

Are you all ready for the funeral procession to the tomb?

I think so.

- The mummy is carried to the tomb in a procession.

- Musicians, dancers and priests follow the mummy.

- Sometimes mourners are paid to cry loudly as they follow the coffin.

- Some processions travel by boat along the river Nile.

65

Stele
a stone monument

Robes
made of linen

Perfumes
and oils
which are needed in the next life

Censer
An incense burner

1
sceptre

2
headrests

3
cat
statues

So what happens now?

Is this the afterlife?

No.

There are some more rituals inside the tomb.

This is the ceremony of the opening of the mouth.

- The Egyptians believe that the deceased need to be able to eat and drink in the afterlife.

- This ceremony makes sure that they can take food and water.

- There are 75 stages to the ritual.

- The priest touches the mouth of the mummy with different tools.

There are so many hieroglyphs on the walls.

What are all these little men for?

Those are **shabti**, the servants who carry out work for the deceased in the afterlife. They are made from clay, wood, wax, stone, terracotta and even glass. Some of them are shaped like mummies and have spells written on them. Others are made with tools for the work they would do, for example baskets and farming tools.

Design a shabti

Draw your own shabti.

What tools would it need to do your work for you?

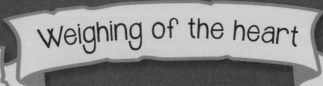

Weighing of the heart

There is one more ceremony.

So is this person in the afterlife now?

Before the dead person can finally enter the afterlife, the gods will judge if he has had a good life.

I've heard about this place. Inside the Hall of Maat the god Anubis places your heart onto a scale with a feather.

If the heart is light you pass into the afterlife.
But if your heart is heavy, the crocodile god Ammut eats you up.

Back to where they began

Quiz questions

1. Which of these is a type of jar that holds organs during mummification?

   a) chocolate
   b) canopic
   c) cryptic

2. Who is the god of the Underworld?

   a) Osiris
   b) Ra
   c) Isis

3. Which river runs through the centre of Egypt?

   a) the Thames
   b) the Nile
   c) the Jordan

4. What is the name of the black make-up used to decorate eyes?

   a) kohl
   b) coal
   c) curl

5. Where was the capital of Egypt during the New Kingdom?

   a) Thebes
   b) Memphis
   c) Cairo

6. What is the name for an Egyptian king?

   a) baron
   b) sultan
   c) pharaoh

7. What is the heart measured against during the ceremony of the weighing of the heart?

   a) a scarab beetle
   b) a feather
   c) a sandal

8. What is papyrus used for?

   a) making paper
   b) making an omelette
   c) making balloons

Answers

pp. 22-23

pp. 36-37

IFYOUCAN
TRANSLATE
THISPAGEYO
SYREVERAU
TADELLIK
READINGHI
EROGLYPHI
ODLLEWSC
NE

IF YOU CAN
TRANSLATE
THIS PAGE
YOU ARE VERY
SKILLED AT
READING
HIEROGLYPHS
WELL DONE

pp. 66-67

p. 75

1. b) canopic
2. a) Osiris
3. b) the Nile
4. a) kohl
5. a) Thebes
6. c) pharaoh
7. b) a feather
8. a) making paper

How did you do?

GLOSSARY

Adze
(adz)
a carving tool

Akhet
(ak-het)
the season
June-September

Amulet
(am-yoo-let)
a lucky charm

Ankh
(ank)
a symbol which
meant 'life'

Archaeology
(arc-ee-ol-o-gee)
the study of ancient
objects and places

Canopic jar
(can-o-pick jar)
jars that hold
organs during
mummification

Cartonnage
(car-ton-age)
linen or papyrus
which could be
moulded to make
masks

Cartouche
(car-toosh)
a name plate for
the dead

Censer
(sen-ser)
an incense burner

Henna
(hen-na)
a dye made from a
plant also called
henna

Hieroglyphics
(hy-ro-glif-icks)
ancient Egyptian
writing

Kohl
(koll)
black eye make-up

Menit
(men-it)
a musical
instrument

Natron
(nay-tron)
salt used in
mummification

Ochre
(o-ker)
a red mineral used
in make-up

Papyrus
(pap-eye-rus)
a plant used for
making paper

Peret
(per-et)
the season
October-February

Peseshkaf
(pe-sesh-kaf)
a blade with a
forked end

Pharaoh
(fair-oh)
the name for the
rulers of ancient
Egypt

Pyramid
(pirra-mid)
a triangular
burial tomb

Sarcophagus
(sar-kof-a-gus)
a decorated coffin

Sceptre
(sep-ter)
an ornamental staff

Shabti
(shab-tee)
a figurine which
would carry out
work in the afterlife

Shemu
(shem-oo)
the season
March-May

Sheneb
(shen-eb)
a trumpet made
of silver or gold

Shroud
(shrowd)
a cloth covering
for a dead body

Sistrum
(sis-trum)
a musical
instrument

Stele
(steel-a)
a carved stone
monument

Tomb
(toom)
a place where the
dead are buried

About the author and illustrator

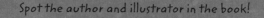

Spot the author and illustrator in the book!

Frances is a historian and dedicated castle visitor. She can usually be found in the library surrounded by stacks of books that she can't wait to read.
Likes: Books, holidays, thunder storms, trains and the theatre
Dislikes: Washing up
Favourite Colour: Purple
Favourite Food: Fish and chips
Favourite Places: Libraries and castles

Grace is an illustrator and animator. She has two dogs Muffin and Kodie-bear and they love to explore together.
Likes: Adventures, the ocean, fairy lights, olives and animals
Dislikes: Having wet socks
Favourite Colour: Turquoise
Favourite Food: Apple crumble
Favourite Places: Forests and outer space

Published by b small publishing ltd. www.bsmall.co.uk © b small publishing ltd. 2017

Text copyright © Frances Durkin 2017   Illustrations copyright © Grace Cooke 2017

• 1 2 3 4 5 • ISBN 978-1-911509-09-7 •

Published by Sam Hutchinson   Production by Madeleine Ehm   Printed in China by WKT Co. Ltd.